Frankly Speaking About
Widowhood

Frankly Speaking About

Widowhood

DEALING WITH LOSS AND LONELINESS

BETH E. WALLACE

Frankly Speaking About Widowhood:
Dealing with Loss and Loneliness

Published by Wheatmark®
1760 East River Road, Suite 145,
Tucson, Arizona 85718 U.S.A.
www.wheatmark.com

ISBN: 978-1-60494-931-5 (paperback)
ISBN: 978-1-60494-935-3 (ebook)
LCCN: 2012955379

In Memory of
Dennis Hunter Wallace
1940–2007

Contents

Introduction

This book is not about solutions. It's about letting you know that you are not alone in the feelings you are experiencing now that you have been widowed. Lots of books will tell you how you should feel, how you should deal, how you should kneel, but let's get real and talk about our real experiences—the things that make us sad, make us mad, our fears, our needs, our wants, our guilt; things that make us cry and sometimes even make us laugh. Many secular books write about real feelings and, unashamedly, intimate situations, but Christian books seem to ignore or gloss over our private inner problems—the turmoil that tears us up and leaves us feeling guilty, depressed, but mostly alone.

   I am not an expert, not trained in counseling, and not always the Christian example I would like to be. I am not offering a formula for healing your wounds, but I have been there, and I have spoken with others who are also traveling this path. I want to share our experiences with you so that you know you are not alone in this struggle. I want you to know that even believers who know in their hearts that the Lord walks beside them in this valley have the same feelings of abandonment, loss, and doubt that others experience. I want you to know that it is okay to have these feelings, and that they may even be helpful in sorting out your life and your future. They say you can allow the disappointments and trials in life to make you bitter—or better. I vote for better!

As a Christian going through the process of suffering loss, I have felt emotions that I found no outlet for and experienced guilt over. I have also realized my advantage in having a relationship with God that I could hold on to during this difficult time in my life.

I hope that my willingness to share my innermost feelings might encourage you to lift up your head, realize you are not alone in this struggle, and help you to seek a new direction for your life.

Hold on! It's a bumpy ride.

Immediate
Reactions
and Actions

AFTER THE LOSS OF A SPOUSE

Shock!

No matter how prepared you think you might be, the death of a spouse is a shock that will leave you numb and bewildered. Whether your loss came after a long illness or a sudden incident, you will find yourself in this disconcerting state. Whether you had a good and loving marriage or a miserable and abusive one, you will still have a lot to deal with. Some of your thoughts and actions might surprise or alarm you. Some of the unknowns you face may overwhelm you. Some of your feelings and actions may make you feel guilt, and you may even question your walk with God. But you are still in shock. Give yourself time to adjust and regroup. It takes a while to get back on track and start walking solo when for so long you have had a spouse with whom to share burdens and make decisions. Realize that your God has broad shoulders and a love for you that is beyond your understanding. He will not only wait for you to get back on track; He will help you each step of the way if you let Him. He will help you even when you don't realize it.

On top of your shock and numbness, you are bombarded with all manner of decisions that you must make immediately. The first year of widowhood is so demanding, you often don't really feel your loss until the dust settles. (I found the second and third years to be the hardest.) If you have planned for this scenario ahead of time, it is still a difficult, confusing, and demanding experience. However, if you have never taken an active role in decision making, not planned financially and practicably for your future—or maybe never been the one responsible for paying bills and making the decisions in your marriage—you have a lot to learn and deal with. I know some widows who had never written a check, did not know what their assets were, and had no clue where to start. Many women never learned to drive or had driven so seldom, they had lost their driving skills. Some had no clue about household maintenance (and no desire to learn). Men who are widowed often are bewildered about how to do their laundry and cook a meal. They either go out to eat a lot or find a new lady fast—which is often a bad move.

I was fortunate. My husband and I had planned for this situation. My husband was twelve years older than me, and he wanted to be sure I could stand on my own when the time came. We also had experienced the care and loss of our parents, which gave us some idea of the decisions that needed to be made ahead of time.

I have tried to tell others that they need to plan for this scenario in advance, but people tend to put these things off or refuse to deal with them at all. Planning ahead may seem strange; it will cost you time, money, and effort, but believe me, it saves you in the future. Just having your ducks in a row helps when the time comes.

If you are reading this book as a widow, you may already have discovered what you should have done; however, having experienced what you have, you still need to plan for your future and encourage others to plan ahead. Your family will appreciate your thoughtfulness in its time of loss.

Some things to consider:

Estate planning

Have a will in place. Once your life settles a bit, get a new will drawn up to reflect your new situation. List items you want to leave to certain people, so there are no questions as to your wishes (they are *your* belongings after all).

Funeral planning

Many think this is morbid; however, it is so much easier on the family and less expensive to have this taken care of ahead of time. You know what you've been through. Encourage others to be prepared.

Financial planning

It is never too late to organize what assets you have and to protect them for the future. If you are left with an income, you need to use it wisely; if you have little to work with, you need to make some definite plans.

Talk about your personal plans with your family and leave written instructions so there are no doubts as to your desires. Your family may not want to hear it now, but they will appreciate it later. Take time now to let your loved ones know that you love them, so that you don't leave them with regrets for missed opportunities.

Death is a shock. We all come to this one day, so we need to be prepared not only for the material aspect, but especially for the spiritual aspect. It is never easy to face the loss of a loved one, but take comfort in knowing that our loved ones have a new life with the Lord and are waiting for us to join them. Life on this earth is brief in eternity terms and eternity is … well, for eternity.

We will discuss this more in a later chapter, but even through this rough time, keep your trust in the Lord. If you question a loved one's salvation and feel a terrible uncertainty about their fate, you must leave it in God's hands. Anne Graham Lotz (Billy Graham's daughter) wrote in her book *Heaven My Father's House* that she tells families who are unsure of the salvation of a loved one who has died that they can trust the Judge of all the earth to do right. We do not always know the heart of another or what they have experienced with God, but we must trust that our God is big enough to handle it.

Let me say this: *what you cannot change you must accept, but you can determine your own faith and influence others.*

Reality

I don't want this kind of reality, but what choice do I have? I can either decide to deal with it or crawl into a hole of self-pity.

First we need to give ourselves some time to recoup. We have been through a heartrending experience, and there is much to do to reorder our lives.

I recently heard that when your spouse dies, you must remake/redefine who you are and what your goals are. All you centered your life around was in terms of a couple. You did things to complement the efforts of your spouse. You planned your day as a couple, whether doing activities together or separately, and then coming back together at the end of the day. But all activities were about your lives as a couple or a family. When your spouse is no longer there to consider, and your family is grown and on its own, what do you do?

Some will try to fill up every minute so they don't think about it; others don't want to do anything till the numbness passes. Either in the extreme can hurt you, but there are times when both are helpful.

I often wonder what the purpose of my going on is—maybe it's for this reason right here: to share a few words of comfort and hope with someone else who is going through their time of loss, searching, and repurposing. God knows, and I guess that should be enough for me.

Anger

Here are some of my journal entries about my anger:

- The next time someone tells me "it gets easier with time," I'm going to tell them, "No. It doesn't—you just have to learn to accept it." I miss Dennis more each day it seems. Every day I am reminded of what we had together and wish I had appreciated it even more.

- ANGER. I talk about Dennis a lot, and I guess people get tired of it—but I need to talk about him just as they do their spouses and families.

- ANGER. A young woman died today. Why? Why is it some die just when life is beginning? Why do some linger long after the fall foliage is gone, while others die in the spring of their lives or in full bloom?

- ANGER. People ask, "How are you?" You say fine, okay, hanging in there—but inside you are saying "NOT!"

Just before my husband died, he said please don't hate me after I die. Gee, why would he ever think I could hate him for dying? I told him at the time I wouldn't ever feel that way. It was a privileged to have had him—even when he was sick. I couldn't be angry with him—it wasn't his choice to get cancer.

I may not want to admit it, but I have been angry with him, and I have caught myself asking: why did you have to die and leave me all alone?

I am angry at the loss of our plans and dreams, with all the things I had and may never have again.

Ashamedly, I have been angry with him and with God for the circumstance I find myself in. I've even found myself wishing we had died together in the auto accident we should not have walked away from two years before he became so ill.

I'm angry with people who are too busy to care and others who don't know this kind of loss—yet hand out glib advice. People who think now that you don't have someone to care for that you are free game to serve them or their agendas.

I am angry with people who take their own life for granted and throw away their own precious relationships for shallow demands.

I am angry with people who keep you from experiencing new activities and services for others because they want things their way only. I am angry with people who don't care about my feelings, my disappointments, and my loneliness. I am angry with people who can't find something bad to say about you, so they make something up; people who say to others, "I'm concerned about so and so being alone," yet never once have they called and offered their company. (Hey, I guess I am angry.)

Many years ago, we had some difficulties (as all families do) with rebellious teenagers and aging parents. People asked if the situation made me mad at God. No, I said. God is not the cause of the problem. We make choices in this life, and we are accountable for them — not God. Yet so often we do blame Him.

So am I angry with God because He allowed my husband to suffer and die right when we had reached a point that most folks begin to enjoy time together?

Well, I wasn't at first. I spent a lot of time with God that first year, and that helped me get through the shock. But now, several years later and with multiple disappointments and closed doors that have magnified my loneliness and unhappiness, I have to admit that there are times I have been angry with God. I know that we are promised that all things are meant for our growth and not our harm (James 1, Jeremiah 29:11). In the storms of life, we need to put our trust in Him. Sadness, loneliness, and discouragement are compounded by time, and, as with all impatient human beings, one wonders when the sorrow will end.

When will things start to look up? When do I get a break? If I can't be this/that, can't do this/that, what do I do and how long before I get to do it? If I am to have a new chapter in my life, another bond with someone, will it come before I'm too old to care? If not, what can I fill my life with?
I have reached so many roadblocks.
When, where, and what am I to do now?

Frankly, I don't believe God turns His back on our anger. Sometimes anger stimulates our communication with Him. Maybe anger is one way we express our feelings and work out our relationship with Him by sharing all aspects of our life with Him. Still we can get so angry with our supposed wrongs that we blame God or turn our backs and rebel against Him.

We also do this same thing to Him when our lives are running smoothly and things are so good that we forget about Him. Sometimes God has to turn us around to get our attention, and sometimes He just waits for us to turn back to Him.

So back to the original question.

Am I angry? Am I angry with God because of my circumstances?

Well yes. I have felt angry at my situation, but not as often and, as time passes, not as desperately. As for God, I know that I live in this world and therefore have to deal with the things this world brings. I know that while my Lord does not always take sorrows out of our lives here, He never makes us walk through them alone. Others may fail us; He never does. I still hope that I keep reaching to Him and not turn my back on Him. Yes, I have been angry, but I think I am starting to get over it. I am learning to accept what I cannot change and go on with my life. I hope that He soon enables me to see His plan for the rest of my life, but if not, I pray I will learn to accept His answer— yes, no, or wait until God's time.

Fears

How Can I Do This by Myself?

Can I make decisions?

Yes, but you need to learn the process, and that may take some time, assistance from others, and a dose of self-confidence. Don't rush into situations that can wait. Learn patience, listen to advice, seek answers to questions, and then make decisions based on all the facts you have collected. Don't expect someone else to make all your decisions; you may not like what they decide, and *you* are the one who will have to live with those decisions.

Can I learn to be self-sufficient?

Give some things a try, and you may surprise yourself. If it is a task you know you are not capable of or knowledgeable enough to tackle, hire someone you trust, or ask someone who has offered to help you. Just don't continually expect someone's help. Save their offer of help for things you absolutely cannot do.

Who do I trust?

Be cautious. There are those who will intentionally take advantage of your situation and emotional state. Also, sometimes well-meaning individuals offer advice or services they are not really qualified to give. Sometimes it is better to pay a qualified person to do a proper job in the first place, than to pay them more later to repair further damages. Ask people whose opinion you trust for recommendations of financial institutions, law firms, realtors, individual repairmen, or companies they have used and were satisfied with. Ask a friend to go with you to appointments. As you are aware, because of the chaos in your life, you may not feel you are thinking clearly, and it is good to have a second pair of ears to hear what you may miss. Prepare written questions ahead of time and write down answers. It will take less time, and you won't forget to ask the important details. Take time to weigh your decisions carefully, and don't sign any document you have questions about.

Money

My husband saved for our retirement and to ensure I would have adequate income if something happened to him. He was afraid that family and friends in need might take advantage of me and drain my savings. This happens far too often for many widows. We help our children beyond what we should, or we remarry and do not carry out good financial planning and protection. In some cases, unscrupulous people help themselves to our hard-earned funds. It is a cause for concern.

It's hard not to help our kids when they are in a jam, though sometimes it is our responsibility to help when there is a legitimate need and if we have the funds to do so. However, it is also our children's responsibility to not take advantage and not ask for frivolous things. Adult children are adults and need to solve their own problems just as we had to. If we continually run to their aid, they will never really grow up. While we do not want them to struggle, we also need to protect our future and theirs by not draining the funds that will support us in our final years. I have helped not only my kids, but also friends and church members where I could, but I try not to do it out of funds that I will need to support myself.

My kids are out there working hard to support their families, but there are those who are using their folks for a free ride. Helping someone who won't help themselves is not loving. Who will do it for them when your money runs out? When it does, who will take care of you? Use your resources prayerfully and mindfully.

Should you enter into a new marital relationship, you need to discuss your financial situations and your plans together. It is not your children's property and money, it is yours to use wisely. You will want to discuss how your estates will be fairly divided and what personal items will pass on to whom. If you are not willing to be open, aboveboard, and discuss this, you might want to reconsider remarriage. Someone who truly loves you and wants a good marriage should not only be open to discussing these matters with you, but should be happy to do so to protect his family interests as well as yours.

Today we are constantly bombarded with agencies, ministries, organizations, and individuals who are asking for donations. While many of these are legitimate needs, some are scams, and we need to be wise in decisions to donate money. If you want to help someone, *you* choose who to give to, how much, and how often. Do not give in to high-pressure techniques and constant pleas. Remember, you are alone and vulnerable too, so you need to say no when you cannot give (and not feel guilty about it).

Then there are those who are lurking around the corner to try and drain you of money and assets for themselves. Do not give personal information to people you don't know; do not accept phone solicitation (say no or just hang up); and do not leave your purse and ID where others can help themselves. These people are clever. Be alert!

How can I stand the silence?

Make noise! Don't isolate yourself. We all need times of quiet contemplation, but we also need times of involvement in life. Turn on your radio. Do physical activities. Join in activities you enjoy even if doing so seems sad at first.

I'm afraid to live alone ...

This is a big one—especially if you have never lived alone. Doing so is fearful! Maybe you can't cope with being alone. Talk with family and friends and seek solutions. Maybe you will need to live with someone, but really think this through, as it not only affects your life, but those you live with. Maybe you will need to move into an environment where you feel safer. Maybe you will have to do some things to your present home that help you feel more secure (see Things That Go Bump in the Night chapter).

I am fearful of the unknown ...

We all are, but we can hold to the promise of God: "I will never leave you." Don't let life overwhelm you; take it one day, one step at a time.

Decisions I Must Make Now

It is not wise to make snap decisions regardless of your situation. However, when your spouse dies, you are often forced to make some decisions right away and when you are feeling emotionally vulnerable. Be careful. If you have not planned ahead for this scenario, you will have to do so now.

Funeral arrangements/follow-up

Don't allow others to talk you into extravagant arrangements that you really do not have the funds for. Your spouse would not have wanted you to do this. With family and the funeral director, plan a respectful, simple funeral that will honor your loved one's memory. You do not have to impress others.

Can I live in my house/location?

You will need to consider your options and do what your income and your circumstances permit. Give yourself time; do not make hasty decisions. On the other hand, do not stay in a situation that will drain you monetarily and emotionally.

Do I have enough money?

Look at your situation and write out a budget and a plan for your future.

Do I need to work?

Some will choose to work or continue working, not only for financial reasons, but to keep busy and active. Others may not need to work at a job, but if this is an option, find activities that help fill some of your time and get you out of the house.

Short-range plans

Short-range plans are important so that you do not make snap decisions and waste your assets. Clear up debts so you may start with a clean slate. Keep a list of all your sources of funds. Take your spouse's name off of all accounts and contact the three major credit bureaus[1] to

---

1   Experian, P.O. Box 2002, Allen, TX 75013, 888-397-3742;

tell them that your spouse has passed away; this will prevent others from using his credit without your knowledge.

Be careful using credit cards. It is easier and safer to use cards than carrying cash; however, we are not always safe from *ourselves*. It is easy to run up your bill without realizing it until the shock at the end of the month. Keep track of your charges; don't go beyond what you can pay monthly. Pay your card off each month rather than making partial payments, which add up interest charges.

If you still have financial obligations, budget your money to cover your payments and daily expenses, plus protect your future. You may need assistance in refinancing or renegotiating terms. Ask someone you trust to go with you to appointments as a second pair of ears, and then use that person as a sounding board to help you with your decisions.

Long-range plans

Talk with your tax person, financial counselor, banker, insurance agent, and others who handle your accounts and investments to help plan for your future needs. Take sound advice,

---

Equifax Credit Information Services, Inc., P.O. Box 740256, Atlanta, GA 30374, 800-685-1111; TransUnion LLC, P.O. Box 2000, Chester, PA 19022, 800-888-4213

but don't be pushed into rush decisions. Choose the best plan for you.

Each of us faces a different financial scenario but all are vulnerable at this time of tremendous change. Even people who are fully aware of their assets and business situations can make foolish decisions that cost dearly. Take time to check out the facts, which will help you to make wise decisions.

If you can afford to, look into long-term-care insurance and solid investments that will protect your assets. Consider putting aside money in gold and silver, and put those assets in a safe-deposit box. Check out any agent or company you deal with, and don't make snap decisions. If it sounds too good to be true, it probably is.

If your mortgage and major bills are paid up, rather than buying life insurance that you pay for but never see, consider making your own funeral arrangements ahead of time. By taking care of your final expenses and *keeping out of debt*, the money and assets you leave will all go to your family without obligations.

Feelings

FEARS - FACTS - FICTION

Regrets/Guilt

I was not sure what I wanted to do when I graduated from high school, so I attended school to become a licensed practical nurse (LPN). For a number of reasons, I didn't particularly care for nursing so did not finish. However, circumstances required me to work, and I spent many years working as a nurse's aide in hospitals and nursing homes. When I finally was able to get into a different line of work, I thought I would never have to go back to caring for the sick and dying. Little did I know that this was only preparing me for what lay ahead.

When my parents reached their eighties, they both suffered severe health problems and injuries. Each had to be cared for physically and emotionally. My dad had Parkinson's and broke his hip. After the fracture, he was in a care facility close to my home, but I spent almost every evening tending to his physical and financial business. I loved my dad and to see him deteriorate was difficult. His mind was still good, but his body just froze up and wasted away. Between working full-time, looking after my mother, who was in a nearby retirement center, and my dad in the nursing home, I had little time for my own life. I was exhausted and frustrated with continually having to care for things that my parents were paying these facilities a lot of money to do. But they were my parents; I loved them and wanted them to be treated right. My poor husband, who began having his own health issues, was burdened with taking up the slack at home in addition to meeting his own parents' needs. It was not a good life. I wanted to do the best I could for my dad, but you can only stretch so far. I was overwhelmed, running for medicine, doctor appointments, and financial business on top of working and running my own home.

Though I was at the facility almost every night, I rarely got to actually visit with my dad. Someone was always pulling me out of the room to sign this and attend to that. One day I told the nursing home I would not be in the following evening. I needed a break—but the home called me at work to request I bring in some medication they had run out of. *So much for a break.* On that particular day, my dad was very ill and confused. I began to see him as a patient and myself as a caregiver. As I left the home, I was in tears of sorrow and frustration. I remember saying, "God, if you aren't going to cure him, take him home. I just can't stand this."

A couple of days later, my dad called me on the phone, and in his familiar voice, he said, "I just wanted to thank you." When I asked him what he was thanking me for, he said, "Just for everything you've done." I told him, "That's okay, Dad. Love you. See you tomorrow after work." The next day I got a call at work to take him to the emergency room. There my husband and I sat with him for three full days and nights, caring for him, and watching him die.

In the next year, my husband Dennis was diagnosed with prostate cancer; then my mom broke her arm, then her femur. Both of Dennis's folks (who lived two blocks away) were also having severe health problems. Unable to stay alone, my mom went to the same facility where my dad had been, but she was extremely unhappy there. It was decided that it would be better to build onto our house and to bring her home.

Dennis (bless him) retired at age sixty-two, had his first surgery, and then took on the job of full-time caregiver. With the three parents he was dealing with, this was no easy task. Each had a stubborn streak a mile long. However, for the next couple of years while I was still working, we managed okay. Then things took another downward turn. Dennis's dad was injured and passed away, his mother suffered a fall and a concussion that left her angry and confused, and my mother, who was both arthritic and had osteoporosis, started suffering from collapsed vertebra. No one felt good, no one was happy, and everyone needed attention. I believe my mom had a stroke, even though the doctor appeared reluctant to confirm it. The last few weeks of her life, she required total care, and between Dennis and myself, she got it; though once again, I felt I was separating her from being my mom to being a patient. She died at home in 2004.

In December of 2005, I was finally able to retire. Dennis and I looked forward to traveling, camping in our trailer, working on our hobbies, and enjoying each other's company. But that summer I developed a large abdominal tumor and Dennis started having health issues. By the time I had the benign tumor removed, Dennis was diagnosed with leukemia and had to undergo massive chemo treatments. Chemo kills the body's immune system, and, within days of the treatments, he suffered from multiple infections and had no will to go on. He was so violently ill, in fact, that he wanted to just die, but for my sake, he continued treatment. He was in the hospital 190 days between January and October, and all but four of the days he was not hospitalized, he went to the cancer center for blood work and treatment.

Once again I became the caregiver, spending all day fixing medications, cleaning his port tubes, coaxing him to eat, taking him to the clinic, battling the medical system (which is the worst part), and wondering why all this was happening. At the end, they removed his eye due to infection, and I knew he would never recover. I was unable to bring him home as I had promised him, so I spent every day with him at the hospital. I would go home at night totally spent, and feeling guilty for leaving him alone. Dennis passed away in October 2007.

Now I tell you all this, not so you'll feel sorry for me, but to stress my being both a loved one and a caregiver and how I had to separate the two existences. I suppose if I had not seen my loved ones at some point as patients, I would not have been able to do the things I had to do for them. I gave them shots, cared for their wounds (which was a painful process), cleaned, and spoon-fed them. Unbe-knownst to me, the nurse's training I received in my youth gave me the ability to perform these tasks. I suppose I was separating emo-tionally, and God was preparing me for their loss. Still, I felt guilty because I wanted God to take them home. Then I felt guilty when He did.

Since then I have learned that this is a natural reaction many people have when there is an impending death. However, knowing so and accepting it as normal are two different things.

As a Christian, I felt guilt for allowing the various thoughts and feelings in, and for not acting or reacting as I felt a good Christian should. I was ashamed at my emotional out-bursts and for being short-tempered with the people around me.

I felt guilty when I wondered if I could have done more. Could I have been more patient, more understanding, spent more time with them, loved them better?

All three of them were Christians, and I will see them again someday. All three of them knew that I loved them and that I was only human with limitations. All three of them suffered terribly at the end, and I wanted them to be with the Lord instead of suffering. But exhausted and frustrated, I felt guilty and selfish for feeling that way.

I have soul searched and researched many opinions on this matter. I have concluded that I must believe that I did the best I could at the time and let God handle the rest.

Loneliness

No one knows loneliness until they have been there.

I recently read in an article on loneliness that the Bible portrays hell as a form of loneliness. And loneliness is certainly a hell. The loneliness I experienced made me want to be sure that I spend eternity with others in heaven.

I can at least look forward to being with the Lord, His angels, and those who placed their hope in Him.

When you are widowed, you find that even crowds can be lonely places—at least in this life.

The same article states that the pain of being alone causes you to feel emotional pain, rejection, and bad about the company it leaves us with. (Meaning ourselves!)

Sometimes we are our own worst enemy when it comes to loneliness. People don't mean to exclude us; we are the ones who feel different and out of sync. Just like any wound, it takes time to heal—allow yourself the time. We are the ones who must change how we feel, but this takes work and time.

Sometimes people do say careless, unfeeling things to you. I have resented people telling me that I should learn to like my own company or that I should learn to stay home and be content—*well thank you very much!* No one knows how lonely it is to sit alone, eat alone, and go to bed at night alone in a big lonely house.

It really isn't any of their business, and I don't have to let their ignorance of a situation affect me. I hope that they don't have to learn this lesson the hard way. No one can really do anything to help (all the time), but please don't make it worse for me by saying, "Get used to it."

When things go wrong in life, it is easy for someone else to say, "Be patient—all in good time. God will take care of it in His time, not yours." It is easy for others to be optimistic when things are going well for them, but it doesn't help you much when your life is falling apart.

God is in control. God takes care of us. Yet we also live in a world that is Satan's domain, and suffering is part of this life. We can't always just get used to it, learn to live with it, or be patient during it. However, we can learn not to let this life control us, and we can learn not to let peoples' attitudes dominate us. We have a right and a need to work out our feelings no matter how long it takes.

However large or small your loss may be, it is your loss, and you need time to deal with it. Many suffer loss through different situations in life: divorce, broken friendships, loss of health and independence, loss of a pet, a job, a home. All loss takes time to heal.

We should not minimize loss in others. However, some people who can't seem to handle their loss need encouragement to get beyond the pain and resume living.

Sometimes we spend so much of our time dwelling on memories of our past or dreaming about the future that we miss the things of today. Do we long for our memories because when they were happening, we didn't take time to enjoy the experience? Do we miss the things of today because we are too busy looking at tomorrow? My dad used to say, "You're wishing your life away." How true. Thinking tomorrow would be better than today, I missed the best times of my life.

I've taken trips where I was so anxious to get to the next attraction that I missed out on the current one. My vacation was over too quickly, and I didn't realize what I had really seen until I later looked through my photos.

A product of our times, we rush here and there and hurry through tasks, neglecting quality, fulfillment, and contentment. Our children grow up and move away, and we wonder what happened. We're young and suddenly we're old and wondering how we missed it all. What was once so important has no value today, yet we keep living in a spin. Instead of growing where we are planted, we blow in the wind. We learn only after it is too late.

Even during life's difficult times, we can find things, relationships, and experiences that someday we may remember as special.

Savor your moments!

Self-image

A lot of how we react to a loss comes from our own self-image—well maybe not the loss reaction, but where we go after a loss. You need to feel good about yourself to start looking to the future. This is not easy, especially when your whole world has fallen apart. Those who have self-image issues to start with face a difficult task, and it will take time.

Seek support and help from others who have been there. Help can come from those trained to help, direct, and encourage you through your difficult time. Sometimes help can come from a friend who is just willing to listen. But realize your healing still has to begin within you. Do positive things to get yourself started. Get organized and in control of your life. Take a look at your situation; evaluate your spiritual, financial, and physical needs. Don't neglect what makes you feel and look good.

Writing down schedules, listing assets, dealing with bills, and organizing important papers can all help you know where you are so you can proceed with life.

This is not everyone's cup of tea, but I have found that cleaning out my husband's things, giving shoes and clothes to friends and the needy, distributing keepsakes to his family, packing away some items, and nicely displaying others made me feel I was honoring his memory. This was what I needed to do; others hang onto items for years. But creating a shrine can often prolong the healing process.

Using the funeral book as a memorial book also helped me to heal. I added articles, pictures, poems, and copies of family memorials, etc. Though many pictures and memories brought tears to my eyes, they were tears that needed to flow.

I also spent that first year cleaning out drawers, closets, and boxes that had been packed away for years, generally de-cluttering my life.

I journaled my feelings that first year of being alone. I used this activity to express my feelings, mourn, cry, remember, smile, and heal. Most of all, I found this as a way to commune and be comforted by my Lord.

Things that Go Bump in the Night

Have you noticed how many things you come across that your spouse must have been doing and knew how to do that you don't have a clue about?

I never paid attention to how often he pulled weeds, trimmed plants, checked the oil, or maintained the water in those yucky golf cart batteries (all six of them).

What about that faulty toilet-flushing mechanism? Sure, I could fix it myself on a Sunday afternoon, but first I had to find the right *special* lever. I conked my head on tools in the shed and made two trips to the hardware store with the assurance of a young salesman that, with my bare hands, I could bend the lever to fit. Of course I couldn't, so I measured the angles and headed back to the shed of unknown tools to bend the lever in the vice. I promptly fell down the back stairs, bending the silly thing in all the wrong angles. Well it ain't pretty, but it flushes.

Likewise, those noises you hear—the creaks, groans, rubbing tree branches, varmint noises—when you're alone in the daytime, they make up a virtual concert. But at night when you are alone, they become sounds of a house of terror. When your spouse or someone else is in the house, you usually don't even flinch at these sounds, but alone at night, even familiar sounds can make your heart race, and the unfamiliar can freeze you under your covers.

Before my husband became so ill, there were occasions he had to be away, and sleep eluded me the entire time. I'd stay up late with the TV running and canned goods stacked behind each door to alert me to an intruder. But in the last year of his life, when he spent so much time in the hospital, I would drag myself home so exhausted that I began to sleep without jolting upright with every sound. By the time he died, I had learned the friendly sounds and blocked them out. Still, occasional *strange* sounds spooked me, so I took a gun safety class and bought a .38 just in case.

I am fortunate to live in a fairly safe community, but precautions are always prudent. Have someone you trust with a knowledge of proper safety regulations and codes, make your home as safe as possible. Have tree and bush branches trimmed and cleared from windows, and secure window and door locks. Install motion lights, and keep emergency lights and flashlights handy. Have your appliances (heater, gas, water heater) checked by a professional for safety.

Have good working phones in various locations in the house, not just for safety from outside things but available should you get sick or fall. Do what you need to do to feel as secure as possible in your environment.

Don't leave your purse or valuables in clear sight. Keep a list of emergency numbers, a list of contact numbers, and a list of health problems and medicines in your purse and on your bedside.

Coming home to a dark house is scary. Set a light to come on to greet you. Some people leave a radio playing. Be alert to changes when you drive up, and if there is any concern, call a neighbor or drive away to a public area to call for assistance. Lock car doors when driving, and glance inside the car (front and back seat) before opening the door to get in.

Wherever you live—do all you can to make you and your home feel safe and secure.

Sex

I want it! Not just the physical act, but the intimacy that goes along with it. There is no shame in that. We are physical beings with built-in needs and desires. Look at Genesis; you will see that God created sex before the fall. He told the animals and man to go forth and multiply. God also gave the special gift of intimacy between husband and wife to enjoy. (We ruined it with sin.)

We all want someone to love us; the kind of love you have with one special person who truly loves you—just as you are (we shouldn't settle for anything else). Some people never seem to find this kind of love, and some don't realize what they have until it is gone. I was one of the lucky ones who had it and recognized it for the most part.

Regardless of your marital experience, when your spouse dies, you feel cut off from so much. Two who were united as one now become a stool with a missing leg—off balance. Suddenly you have no one to touch, hold, or be with. Often what you can't have you desire even more. This can lead to situations that do not honor God and lead us into many other problems. When my husband died, I longed for physical intimacy—yet I knew that I did not want someone to meet just my physical desires regardless of the cost. Some feel so desperate they forget to count the cost.

Unfortunately, while some friends think you should get out and sample the wares, others think you should devote all your time to helping others and serving God. After all, He loves you. Yes, I know God loves me—yet as a human being, I long for human arms to hold me. I once wrote in a card to my husband that a good marriage is a sample of the love the Lord has for us. He gives us our spouse to hold us in arms of love—until the time He will hold us in His.

Physical intimacy as God designed it is a gift and a need we as humans seek—but the gift misused, abused, overused, or neglected can lead to sin.

I longed for human touch. Even before my husband died, I longed for physical love. My husband's last years were full of suffering, a broken back, and prostate cancer. The cancer treatments had severely limited our physical relationship.

Still, we could hold one another and have a hand to squeeze "I love you." But in the last year of his life, even that was impossible as his body had become so frail, with tubes running into his arms, hands, and chest, making it so that even a hug brought tears of pain for him and tears of loss to me. Mentally and emotionally, I felt this loss and a terrible need/desire for a physical relationship. I fantasized and dreamed about it, and then felt terribly guilty and told myself to stop thinking about it. But just telling yourself so and wanting these feelings to go does not take away this need.

After he died, I found an even greater emptiness. I now did not even have him in the room—no one there to talk to; no one to share my thoughts with. Other widows agree with me that to sit down to a meal alone and to lie down at night in an empty house, where no one says good night, are two of the most difficult times of the day. It is no wonder so many people find themselves so desperate to find someone right away. Desperately needing human contact, they do things and find themselves in places and situations they would normally avoid: Internet dating, forbidden trysts, bad company, and unwholesome environments. This can lead to fornication, adultery, poor relationships, and bad marriages—all in a desperate attempt to fill the void to be *loved* by someone.

Death of a spouse often occurs at a time in life when a woman is too young to give up the need for intimacy, but too old to be openly desirable in today's world, making her situation even more lonely and depressing. You can go to all kinds of functions and social events to fill up time, but it is hard to go where everyone is coupled up and watch them go home together, while you go home alone to feel an even emptier void.

Christians, whether or not we admit it, have an even more difficult time dealing with sexual and intimate feelings. We experience guilt on top of our need just for thinking about it. We say to ourselves that a real Christian just shouldn't feel this way.

Anger and resentment raise their ugly heads, too. We wonder:

Why me, Lord?
Why did I lose him?
Why don't I have someone?
Why my husband and not that ninety-year-old man over there?
Why someone in love with their spouse and

*not that bitter couple over there who don't
even like each other?*
Why? Why? Why?

When people say trust in Christ, get busy,
learn to live with it—they haven't a clue how
their pat answers hurt and deepen your guilt
and your grief.

What's the matter with me?
I should be happy with what I have.
Do I really trust God to provide?
*Am I sinning by dwelling on my loss and my
desires?*

Does this feeling lessen, or at least this
desperate need? I think so. As with so much
of what you are experiencing, it is an initial
reaction. As time passes, the physical need
mellows, and the panicky feeling passes. You
begin to look at things with a clearer perspective.

Remember that a physical relationship
is a special gift of God given under the
sanction of marriage, and no marriage is
worth entering into until God can bless it. It
is so easy to jump into a relationship for all
the wrong reasons. If we are meant to marry
again, we need to wait on God's timing and

the person He sends into our lives, if that is His purpose for us. If God's plan does not include marriage, we need to pray that He gives us a peace about it.

Remarriage

This is something you will have to decide. Just don't decide in a hurry. Seek God's choice for your life. Take time to really know the person you wish to marry.

As for me, at first I was not interested in a new relationship. In fact, I think people got sick of hearing about Dennis and me as if he were still present. I didn't feel I wanted anyone to replace him.

Then, after some time had passed, I thought, *well maybe I really don't want to spend the rest of my life alone.* (That gives you kind of a panicky feeling.)

Now, five years later and being much more accustomed to living on my own, I think that I can survive the single life. God has a plan, and He will help me fill it either way. He may know that I need to be as I am now, and I just need to learn to be content alone in His embrace. However, if He should bring someone into my life who shares my views and interests, loves God, and loves and respects me, I would be open to either a platonic friendship or, someday, remarriage.

I met a woman who had been widowed for twenty years. She said she had never considered remarriage. Her husband had been the love of her life, and she felt that if she married someone else, it would not be fair to a new spouse, as she would always compare him with her first husband. She was content as she was. That should be our goal—to learn to be content.

Advice of Others

Where do we go for much needed advice when we feel desperate in our loneliness and loss? Do friends really give the best advice? What about professional counselors, medical experts, financial counselors, and spiritual counselors?

And how big a mess can we get ourselves into by listening to the wrong advice?

I once did clerical work in a high school health office, where students came in for help with various problems. I was not professionally trained to give them advice, but I did know enough to direct them to the appropriate individuals for help. I give the same advice to people going through difficult times. While friends can often help and can share from their own experiences, they often are not qualified to give advice that could alter your life. Some are well meaning; others may have their own agenda, but listen with a wise ear and weigh their words carefully.

Financially, you need to take a look at your situation. You may ask a family member or friend to go over your finances with you, but also seek a professional financial counselor from a reputable source to advise you of your options.

If you have concerns about your physical or mental health, discuss them with your physician. It is a good idea to take someone you trust with you so that she can help you remember what the doctor has to say and help you follow through with the doctor's advice. Take a list of your concerns; ask questions about physical, nutrition, and emotional problems. Often when you are suffering a loss, you feel sadness and depression, and many doctors will quickly write a prescription for chemicals you may not really need. "You're depressed," they'll say. Of course you are: you just lost your loved one, and your whole world has turned upside down. Maybe you do need temporary medicinal help, but talk it over with the doctor, and plan your health care together. Your physician can refer you to appropriate professionals for your specific needs.

If you need counseling, seek someone with adequate training and experience in dealing with grief. Support groups are helpful, but remember that they are usually a group of people who are sharing a like experience and are not qualified to advise you; they are just there to support you.

If you feel desperate enough to seek help, do so with a qualified counselor. As a Christian, I believe it is important to seek Christian counselors who can advise us according to our faith. Often secular counselors advise according to the world's standards. Your minister may be trained to council or will know where to send you for help.

Of course your greatest council comes from God. He has gifted people to help you. God can answer your prayers through the physicians and professionals He has provided.

As for family and friends, it is good to share with them, have them there to listen to you, and help you with overwhelming tasks. Often their suggestions are comforting and helpful. Sometimes it is good just to know they're there for you. Their support is vital, but don't wear them out with your needs. Be grateful and appreciative of those who give of themselves to help you. And be ready and willing to reciprocate when their time of need comes.

A Dog Called Victor

You get a lot of advice when you go through loss and loneliness. It was suggested that I get a pet for company, which I resisted for a long time. I'm not a cat person and hadn't had a dog in years. I really didn't want to deal with all the care an animal required. *Sooooo* ... I got a dog anyway, a real cute Yorkie that I named Victor. He looked so cute lying on a pillow sleeping. Of course, his breathing was battery-operated and could be turned off and on at will. My little toy dog looked so real that I was afraid to leave him in my car for fear someone would break in to save him. I told my son I got a dog, and he hurried over to see. He took one look at Victor and then looked at me and said, "That's just sick, Mom." Unfortunately I had to pull the plug on Victor when his breathing mechanism developed an asthmatic sound.

I now have a real dog. For me it was a good decision—the time was right. I found a little black cocker spaniel named Molly that seemed to need me as much as I needed her. Having another living, breathing being in the house, getting up in the morning to let her out, having someone who is happy to see me when I get home, and someone to say goodnight to has been a good thing in my life.

A pet may not be what you need or want, but they can serve a *purpose* we all need—someone to love, who loves us in return.

Meals on Wheels

I have often made a meal, set the table, and sat down to eat, only to take my plate and dump its contents in the trash. Sitting down at the table alone is *real* depressing. Not only have I thought this, but almost every widow I've talked with has said that meals are one of the hardest times of their day. The worst time for me is Sunday after church, when others are going out with family and friends for dinner and afternoon activities. I go home and look at the walls.

Many sit down in front of the TV, go out to eat too often, or snack and don't eat properly balanced meals. It is really hard to care about nutrition when you are depressed. However, if you don't take care of yourself, who will?

You may need to write down what you eat for a while so that you get into a routine of proper meals and nutrition. Eat simple, well-balanced meals at home, and plan meals with friends frequently. If you can afford to dine out with friends, do so a couple times a week to break the monotony of eating alone. Other widows will be glad to go along with your meals-on-wheels evening.

In My Lowest Times

My time of grieving was a difficult journey. I not only lost my spouse, but I ran into many other disappointments during this same time period. I was terribly discouraged. I wrote the following entries in my journal at some of my lowest points. I share my feelings so that you know that you are not alone in the thoughts you may be experiencing.

Discouragement

Sometimes I wonder if I have a future. Everything I try to do to restart my life runs into a brick wall. Is it God telling me to wait or Satan trying to defeat me and make me doubt?

I need to trust God, and I know I can't give up. But so much has been taken from me with nothing to fill those voids that I frequently become discouraged.

My sisters, my children, and a few friends have

remained loyal to me. I have a home and an income that I am grateful for, but so much of my life has been disrupted that I am discouraged.

On top of my loss in death, I had one disappointment upon another as I tried to go on with my life.

I had hoped to fill the void in my life with service to other Christian sisters, but this proved futile. Rather than the group's leaders taking what I offered to enhance their programs, they saw me as a threat to their control.

Strange how people react. As long as you are weak, vulnerable, and stay in line, they'll drain you dry, pat you on the head, and sit you in the corner. Yet anything you suggest new to enhance existing programs, or anything to jump-start the dull drums of old routines, and you suddenly become a threat and are targeted for destruction. The key is not to allow them to defeat you, but to handle the situation with dignity and integrity.

Disappointment

I felt my church had failed me when my spouse died. Oh, they gave a nice dinner, and many attended the funeral, but they did not give *me* the support I needed *after* the funeral, nor did they give me a chance to grieve and heal.

Many said, if you need anything, call us. When I did call, they made excuses for not being available. I tried to take care of things myself or hired people for the larger tasks, but when I would occasionally have some little thing I could not do myself, no one was ever available. There were times I just sat down and cried.

The youth group at my church wanted to raise money for camp by doing yard work and household chores. I thought I could help them, and they could help me. I was willing to compensate them generously, but their leaders never followed through. It may be just my perception, but people today just don't seem to honor commitments or take the time to help others.

Few people called to check on me after Dennis died, and no one invited me to do anything with them. I tried to keep the lines of communication open by calling old friends, and while they were kind, they just did not have the time or the inclination to spend time with me. I tried to organize other widows for outings, but it just didn't work out. While my husband was sick, a few people did ask if I could use meals. Because I spent most of my time at the hospital or at the clinic, and because he had to be isolated, I thanked them but explained that I had no need at that time. I asked to share a meal later (after his time) when I would need to be with others. Only one couple from my church invited me out for dinner with them, for which I was grateful, but I could have used a lot more of that type of support at the time. Others just didn't take the time or think of doing it.

My church leadership wanted my time and efforts for their programs; however, even though they knew I was going through a difficult period, they never called on me to find out if I was okay or if I could use help. Rather than ministering to my needs at my time of loss, I was expected to act as if nothing had changed. Because I was perceived as a leader, I was expected to be strong, buck up, and attend to tasks—plus do even more now that I had the spare time. People pushed things on me, complained to me, and expected me to do their bidding and do it their way. When I did try to help, they complained, criticized, and gossiped about me.

My daughter ran into one woman who had made demands of me and had fueled the fires of gossip. She asked if I was depressed living alone. My daughter (bless her heart and her quick tongue) told her, "If you are really concerned, it would help if you would call her occasionally." She never did.

I don't mean to sound melodramatic, but nothing hurts more than the toxins you feel from your church brothers and sisters. It's like a sibling who hates you just because you were born. Just like in the world, we are all human and we all make mistakes, but mistreatment from our church family wounds deeply. Church leaders who try to ignore or gloss over problems do no favors to the spiritual well-being of the church. I was so uncomfortable and distracted that I felt I needed to find another house of worship so that I could heal and serve God as I should.

I hope I will treat others traveling this path of sorrow and loneliness with more consideration.

Now I sound bitter. I agree I was deeply hurt, but I write this not just to complain, but to prove a point. We all need to be conscious of what we do and how we treat others—especially when they need us most.

Our churches could provide a valuable service helping prepare people for life's situations. We need to give Christian guidance about marriage, child rearing, handling teenagers, dealing with crisis, dealing with grief, and other losses. We need to prepare people before the trials hit and equip Christian brothers and sisters for organizing their lives and dealing with life's problems. And we need to support them when they need us the most.

Spit in the Ocean

At funerals you'll hear, "If you need anything— just call" and "We'll get together and have dinner soon." While most people mean it, they get busy with their own lives and never call.

It seems that when you need help right away, all you get is a busy signal or no answer. You spring a leak, and no one has time to come. You really need a friend to talk to, and you can't find a soul.

Then you start to think:

Oh, spit in the ocean, who cares anyway?

Why do I bother?
I'm alone and forgotten!
I'm of no importance to anyone.
It's just not fair!
Why do they have everything, and I have nothing?

Is it depression, indifference, resentment, jealousy, or just emptiness?

Well, yes, maybe it is any or all of these, but mostly it is grieving, and grieving needs time for healing and rebuilding. When we allow ourselves to get so down (and there are times we all do), we must not allow Satan to defeat us. This is a time we need to hold to our faith. Change has to come from within us as we partner with time, God, and our own determination to start again.

Do yourself a favor, don't spit in the ocean—there really are others who care. Just give yourself time to find them.

Remember to thank the ones who have helped you and have been there for you. Some are really there for you as often as they can be, but they can't be there all the time. Just don't take advantage of these kind souls.

When you begin to heal and get your life going again, remember to help someone else who is where you have been.

Below are thoughts I wrote in my journal about dealing with others and dealing with my own emotions.

When you feel disappointment, remember:

- When others disappoint or hurt you, don't run away from life. If you have to cry it out, do so. Realize you are just as valuable in God's eyes as are others. Ask Him to give you direction. That may mean you have to take a stand or you may have to make a new start, but whatever you must do, do it with grace and integrity.

- Many in this life will disappoint you. Realize they are only human and have a right to their opinion whether or not they agree with you. No matter how good your intentions might be, they may see it from another angle and may not appreciate your efforts. That's okay, too. You will never please everyone. Just know that you are doing the best you can. When someone wrongs you, remember that you may not like the person, but you must love their soul. Jesus demands it.

- People are different in their way of thinking, in their life experiences, and in their goals for living. Often we just don't understand people's actions. Sometimes they are acting in a self-serving manner; sometimes they just think differently than we do. They may mean no harm, but are just as stubborn as we might be. Even Christians look at things from different perspectives and often want their own way. One way you can handle this is to realize that no matter what someone has done to you or how they live their life, they are just as much God's child as you are. There will come a day when we will all go home to live for eternity with

God, and we will live in harmony. Until then, consider that maybe God wants you to help guide others by an example of forgiveness, tolerance, and love.

- When life's situations don't follow our plan, as author and Bible teacher Joyce Meyer reminds us, "Don't have an opinion where you don't have a responsibility." You don't need to be in charge of everything. In addition, she reminds us, "How long we talk about (linger on, dwell on) our present situations determines how long we will stay in them." (Joyce Meyer Ministries) These are good points to remember. Thank you for reminding me!

Widowhood vs. Divorce/ Good Marriage vs. Bad Marriage

Loss is loss, but losses differ for each individual and for each individual circumstance.

Having been divorced *and* widowed gives me a glimpse of how different and how alike these losses can be.

When I divorced, I felt the loss of a spouse, a father for my kids, a loss of income and security, a feeling of failure, upheaval, anger, hurt, uncertainty, and fear of the unknown. Whether or not one admits it, there is anger at the person whom you feel betrayed you.

Loss in death (of a loved one) brings a terrible depressing loneliness. Whether immediate or down the road, a terrible void cramps your heart. Many of the same feelings hit— the unknown, loss of security, direction. Even if you are one who does experience anger, it usually is at the peripheral things, not the one you loved. He didn't want this loss for you either.

However, everyone experiences loss differently. Many circumstances factor in both scenarios, but for this section, let's look at loss through death of a spouse.

Talk with others who also have lost a spouse, and you will see how differently people deal with their loss. One big factor is the difference between a happy marriage and an unhappy one; for example, a loving and kind spouse or a harsh and judgmental spouse. People who have lost the latter may experience relief and then feel guilt because of it. Yet there is a freedom that comes from no longer being tied to a controlling or critical individual. Still there is a loss of many of the same issues.

Sudden loss or long-term illness also brings varying reactions. Shock, disbelief, denial, fear, long-term sadness, and exhaustion all factor in.

Regardless of the circumstance, each loss differs; each reaction differs. As different as each individual is, each has a right to grieve, to be sad, to search their own heart and thoughts. Each needs time and support of people who respect their right to work through their feelings.

Where Is God
in All This?

Where Is God in All This?

How do people get through grief who don't have God to talk to, to cry with, to hold onto, and maybe even get mad at? It is no wonder people commit suicide, cry themselves to death, run wild, and get themselves into terrible situations in this life—especially if they don't have a relationship with God to give them balance. I have found this to be such a lonely miserable time, but I at least have God to listen to and comfort me.

During this time alone, I gained a new perspective on God and His Word, and I have gained a new understanding of my relationship with Him. I have been in the church all my life. I taught Bible study many years. I've read and heard the scriptures over and over, but since I have been alone, I have really begun to understand my faith. Where once I glossed over Bible chapters, I now see each verse and its wealth of information.

In teaching, I have often remarked how the Bible speaks to each individual at the level he or she needs it to. The Bible stories we heard as children had meaning to us at that simpler stage in life, but as we grew in our walk with the Lord, those same stories became more profound, more meaningful in each stage and situation in our lives. In sorrow, those verses comfort you and mend your heart with the balm of God's love. As sorrow passes, those same words give you focus and hope for tomorrow.

God's word is all-important for our understanding of our world and our purpose. I knew what the Bible said, but never realized how deep it can be if we just take the time to allow the Holy Spirit to guide us. The history, science, and hope for the future are there, and it has only been recently that I have understood its order and completeness. A Bible teacher who I have followed the last few years has given me deeper insight into the real study of scripture, and all the pieces have fallen together.

The Bible teaches us history and science of the creation, the reaching out of God to His wayward children, the promises of God to His people, the faithful pursuit of God's love, the prophecies fulfilled throughout the centuries, the walk of our Lord on Earth to fulfill the promises to the Jewish nation and to be an example for all; then to fulfill the promise revealed in Genesis 3 of the Savior of mankind through His sacrifice of Himself on a cruel cross for our sin. He arose from that grave on that third day and once again bridged the gap of man to God that sin had created. While the Jewish nation was blinded to truth and would not accept Him as their promised Messiah, while they refused to fulfill their task of leading others to Him, He patiently set that agenda aside (for a time) and took one unlikely man (the apostle Paul) to reveal His purpose and plan to *all* the world. By turning to the Lord in trust and faith, by recognizing that through His death, burial, and resurrection, He brought new hope to a sinful and lost world. He breaks the bonds of sin and destruction. So simple a means to have it all; yet much of mankind in his stubborn way continues to deny Him. While this means to salvation is for all— Jew and Gentile—God has not forgotten His promise to the Jewish nation, and the promises revealed from ages past still continue to work to that climax when they will claim Him King of Kings.

This is the Bible in a nutshell. It is the basic outline of a book filled with wisdom and knowledge to reach all ages of history—and *all people*.

So, again we ask, *"Where is God in all this?"*

God does not make us suffer through lone-liness and grief; it is a part of this life. Yet He uses this time to comfort and guide us if we let Him. We don't often remember Him in the good times; we don't delve deeply in the pools of His knowledge when we are distracted by the things of this world and our competitions in life, but when the storms rage, where do we turn? We call out to God, our Creator and Savior—sometimes in anger, fear, uncertainty, loneliness, desperation; sometimes in our need of a true friend, a father, our God.

Healing

REBUILDING THE NEW YOU

Rainbows in the Storms of Life

I never realized what a precious gift I have in my relationship with the Lord. This time alone, time of sorrow, time of disappointment—believe it or not—has been also a time of blessing. My slate has been wiped clean, and my eyes and my heart have opened to His word. Yes, it has been a real rainbow in the storm of my life.

Each of us will find different ways of dealing with our loss, our sorrow, our loneliness, our disappointments, and our healing. Some of us may find new hobbies, vocations, friends, exercise, or other activities we enjoy that help us move on in life. Some may find new relationships, while others may learn to be content on their own. But we all need to decide to begin again and find those avenues that jump-start us.

Journaling

It helped me when I decided to keep a journal the first year after my husband died. This may not be what others would want to do, but doing so was a powerful tool in helping me recover. It helped me realize just how much time I had spent with the Lord, pouring my heart out to Him.

Did He respond? You bet. My journal is proof. On my own I would never have the insights I gained that year—that God was speaking to me, healing me, turning my sorrows into sweet memories, showing me I could go on.

I kept this daily journal for the entire year after Dennis died to document my journey. At other times, I have often written when I felt the need to express my thoughts and commune with the Lord. I find journaling an excellent tool in encouraging my daily devotions.

No one may ever read all my words, but

it is important to me to write them. Through them I hear God's voice, and He directs and heals me with His words.

I am not going to share my many memories of Dennis, as those are *my* memories, just as you have your own memories of your loved one. However, I am going to include portions of my journal entries that express my thoughts about my feelings, my faith, and my God. I hope that they might speak to your heart too.

On Feelings

- Today, I write with tears in my eyes and a hole in my heart. I pray by writing these words—expressing my sorrow—they will be tears of healing and help.

Keeping a journal is not just about writing down your daily activities and good thoughts but expressing your inner feelings. Writing helps you to think things over and better organize your true feelings. Doing so can bring peace of mind and deeper insight.

- I am writing for myself; no one may ever read these words or, if they do, may not understand or care. Yet I need to express how I feel if I am ever going to come to terms with my loss and my loneliness.

I write in journals things I can't explain to others or don't necessarily want to share, but it gives me a constructive way of venting.

- I have so often just gone with the flow rather than taking a serious look at what lay out on the banks and stopping to take advantage of the possibilities. Too often I've dreamed about tomorrow and missed today.

- I've lingered too long on what was and missed out on what could be. I've wanted to be someone else and missed out on being me.

On Faith

- Use situations of life as occasions to cultivate your relationship with God.

- The sun rises every morning; the Son arose once for all.

- If I saw a miracle, would it strengthen my faith? Did all who witnessed the miracles of Jesus believe in Him? Not seeing yet believing, that's faith.

- Faith is not a feeling; it is a commitment.

- Where do you spend your time? If you

want to grow your faith, go where faith is.

- Faith is like a marriage. When you accept God's gift of salvation, the wedding day has occurred; now you work on the marriage.

- Faith I have; trust is harder. I need to work for not just a daily commitment, but moment by moment.

- The Spirit has been with me since youth camp when I declared Christ as my Lord and Savior—whether I have chosen to listen to Him or not. He is there and has directed my path (my conscience) and monitored my thought process to remind me of who I am and what I ought to do (right) in everything. When I don't do right—it is rebellion in me, not failure in Him.

- Yes, I am a Christian—not because of who I am, but because of who I know and put my trust, faith, and hope in.

On Religion

- Dealing with different religious beliefs while we need to be respectful of the beliefs of others, we do not have to give into them. In all, the Word is the final authority. If they can show us in the Bible that we are wrong, we know we must be true to the Word. Jesus was firm in His convictions. When He turned His face toward Jerusalem, He did not allow anyone to delay Him, He did not stay and argue with people, He did not step on others rights, but He lovingly shared truth in word and action. He loved them along the way as we should love others in our path.

- How often does *religion* become an activity, entertainment, or habit, and the relationship with the Lord become non-existent? He is Lord; He is God. He is also our friend who will walk with us, comfort us, encourage us, and show us there is still beauty and purpose as the storms of this life pass. As storms are necessary to replenish life on earth, to renew and grow living things, maybe the storms of our life are necessary to rearrange, renew, and nourish us for the path ahead.

On Recovery

- You've heard people say, "Grow where you are planted." I have learned that I may not like the soil, but I need to accept its nourishment for now.

- I need to remember to hang on. On a day when gray clouds loom (even if it's sunny outside), give it another day. The sun may shine tomorrow. Hang on!

- Why is it we dwell on the regrets of yesterday rather than looking forward to the hopes of tomorrow?

- Take it one day at a time.

- We don't understand the sorrows of this life now, but we will understand someday. When we see Jesus, will we know the purpose of His plan? In the meantime, will we be grateful for its opportunities? Will we have accomplished the tasks? Will we have lived life or merely endured it?

- As the first year ended, I began to notice a subtle change in my attitude. Though I know I will always miss Dennis and his love for me, I still feel him near. For a while, it can create a near panic attack to realize you are all alone—no one to share with, care with, hold you close; this all coming at a particular age when physical and emotional changes are happening that make you feel less desirable and more in need, yet not old enough to be comfortable with that stage of life yet. I wish I were as content with my physical desires as I am with my emotional ones. Because Dennis loved me so much, I still feel that love and bond.

- Several of my friends are also widows, and I can see how different their perspectives are based on the relationship with their partner.

  1. One had a long, loving marriage. She misses her husband, but she is content with her sweet memories and not searching for new ones. She is content with herself.

  2. One friend had a difficult and unloving marriage. While she is not opposed to another relationship, she would only consider it if it was a much different and better one. Otherwise she is content to be on her own.

3. Still another friend seemed to have an on-again/off-again happy/bitter relationship. She seemed overly desperate for another relationship, but her newfound independence may create a block for that.

On God

- Do my bad experiences create doubt and cause me to blame God?

- As with many people, when I question my life situations, I want to blame God for all my woes. I eventually realize that my frustrations often stem from dissatisfaction with myself. When I take time to meditate on my problems, I realize that God does not disappoint me, but I am in too big a hurry for the answers, and when I don't get immediate results or resolution, I become discouraged and blame God for lack of action. Hindsight being better than foresight, I always see that this is not true. God has the better plan or answer. Help me to learn tolerance. Help me not to take everything personally, not be jealous of others, or forgetful that God is in control. Let me rely on Him.

- I often struggle with God over my situations, but once we work through them, I feel better, even if I limp like Jacob did when he encountered and struggled with the angel (Genesis 32:24). Our relationship with God is like struggling in a marriage when there is disagreement; once worked through, it makes the relationship stronger.

- A good marriage is an earthly example of a relationship with God—only He never fails. Through good and bad, you grow closer in understanding, trust, and a common goal. When apart from one another, you feel incomplete. There is something missing.

- You don't get to know someone until you live with him on a daily basis— this includes God.

- Explain why God cannot heal what we deny or cover up. It is not that God cannot heal what we deny, but that He doesn't for our sake because we need to learn and develop from the situation. God could remove my loneliness in one of several ways, but He is not ready to because I am not ready in some way. I still have things to learn, contentment to arrive at, trust in Him to develop, my place in His plan to accept, develop a closer walk with Him, patience to learn, and appreciation to experience. If even I know this, certainly God knows it and so much more.

- God is relentless in His pursuit of us. How far has God gone to get my attention? I ask, "Is that what God is doing? Trying to get my attention?" Is He shouting, pleading with me in the silence and loneliness of my four walls? Did He take away all the distractions so that I would see Him better? I certainly have spent more one-to-one time with Him this year (the year after my husband died). I still don't understand His plan but will take it one step at a time.

- I have so much to be grateful for, but I am always waiting for the next shoe to drop, and it seems like I have had a lot of shoe storms in my life. If God has thrown shoes at me (to get my attention), maybe they will turn out to be blessings. He has always gotten me through those times, and He can make old shoes into warm slippers.

- If God were one of my human friends, would He still be my friend? People only take your unkindness and unfaithfulness for so long. If you don't spend time and energy with them, they drift from your life. Friends tire of your bad moods, your distractions, and your lack of attention. Even a spouse's love will grow cold when he receives no love in return. Yet God remains true, and we treat Him worst of all. We whine and complain, we ignore Him and even curse Him. We take and demand more. We fight against Him. We even shake our fist at Him. How little we adore Him, love Him, glorify Him, worship Him, or be a friend to Him. If a friend treated me like I treat my God, they would be a friend no more. Lord help me to not take your friendship for granted.

- God honors our choices, but we are often willful children who choose a whim, or we stubbornly hold on to what we want—even when we know the choice is wrong. Maybe God lets us have some choices so that we aren't always living in the dream world of *what if* and can move on to *what can be*. I once told a brother in law, an army officer with an attitude, "Wouldn't you rather have men under you that served you out of respect and would go the extra mile for you than ones who fear or dislike you because of what you can do to them, so that they do only what is necessary to get by?" (He didn't think too much of my opinion.) How often is this how we treat God? I think God wants us to serve Him out of our love and respect and from our hearts. He does not want our service because of fear of hell or for what we get out of it. This is the difference between *knowing about God* and *knowing God*. He does not need us. He wants us to want Him.

- God already knows my needs. He wants me to say how I feel.

I ended my journal with some thoughts on how God has blessed my life. These thoughts include:

- My salvation

- My parents and their Christian influence

- My husband who truly loved me and enriched my life

- My children who love me, who love the Lord, and are bringing their own children up to know Him also

- The trials and tribulations He has brought me through. The lessons I've learned that have made me who I am and made me realize that only He can get me through the tough times

- A home for eternity when He is ready to take me there

FOR THESE I THANK YOU
AND PRAISE YOUR NAME LORD

Moving On:
Where Do I Go from Here?

Death of a loved one will never be easy, but we who remain must come to terms with our loss and move on. We read in the book of Samuel that when David realized his son had died, he knew his child could not come back to him, but that he would one day be able to go where his son was. Therefore he got up and went on with his life, despite what had befallen him. There is a message for us there.

Someone once said, "Loss is inevitable; change is optional."

You decide when you are ready and live life again.

Take a look at your own self-worth—read the Word, spend time with God, and become who He created you to be (don't let Satan rob you).

Hebrews 13:5 tells you to be content with what you have, and He promises that He will never leave you or forsake you.

Pray to the Lord; ask Him to take away your burden of sin; free you for service and communion with Him and with those around you.

Turn your eyes upon Jesus and begin to see yourself as Jesus sees you: loved, cared for, unique, and with a purpose.

Seek a purpose for your life. It will do more to help you toward healing than anything else. We all need a purpose.

 Conclusion

So why have I written all this? First I needed to put it in words for my own healing. Maybe by reading my story you will realize that you are not alone in the feelings you are experiencing as you go through this difficult journey in life.

I am no expert; I have no special training. I just want to share my thoughts so that they might help you. Recovering your life after loss is a similar feeling to those who have experienced motherhood. You had no special training; you just found yourself there, and you put forth your best effort.

As we go along this journey of widowhood, we will have good and bad days, and we will face many changes in our lives.

My prayer for you is this:

May the sorrows fade
and the sweet memories linger.
May you have friends that support you
and may you always know that
God is walking beside you.

CPSIA information can be obtained at www.ICGtesting.com
Printed in the USA
LVOW121524100413

328560LV00001B/20/P